two a.m.

Brianne Oliva

BookLeaf Publishing

Presentation by *BookLeaf Publishing*

Web: www.bookleafpub.com

E-mail: info@bookleafpub.com

ISBN: 9789357213011

First edition 2023

hogwarts

cobbled stone ground on a walking bridge
fogged air enter my lungs
grandeur greets me at an ornate metal gate

musty halls and closets stacked high with
shelves
wet grass fields and marble carved pillars
aged books and piles of vials

cold stairs feel warm
warm rooms feel cold
nostalgic photos of some place fly in front of my
face

yet familiarity is so far away

racism

making an entrance causes heads to turn
something glistens in the eyes of the people
more than fear and disgust
a hatred buried deep within
planted by the forefathers of this land

ignorance is blinding
creating the spotlight they imagine shining upon
them
death sits at the beginning and end
of the stories of those who do not look like
the ones that took this land

peaches

pitter patter on the floor
light stratches on the door
opens up and you walk in
i wonder where you've been
all day in the house
napping underneath the couch

digging in your litter
you always seem bitter
but i know you love me
because i can see
the love between cat and owner
is something that no evil can devour

humans

who am i?
who are you?

pronouns
she, he, they
her, his, them

words
used for identifying
not for critizing

we are all made up of the same things
heart, lungs, brain
chromosomes, RNA, DNA

why must there be a right and wrong?
why can't we just be?

i am who i am.
you are who you are.

possibilities

fate smiled above the world
nothing can bring you down
one's heart can clearly see
what is invisible to the eye
head so full of dreams
infinite in form
the beauty of the world
there are so many things
that life could bring

1221

chilled air sweeps against our faces
it is christmas time in nyc
we make our way up to the infamous tree
where lights dance in front of our eyes

this feel like a scene from a movie
we walk up closer through the sea
of people smiling with holiday glee
but all i feel is this moment of us

we ask someone to take our picture
facing the camera as we smile
my heart beats like i've ran a mile
when you kiss me

under the moon
under the stars
between the streets of speeding cars
between all the people

it's just you and me
during christmas in nyc

storm

i feel my mind spin
everything is wrong
spiders are crawling all across my skin
will this feeling stay here for long?

my heart is racing
a hundred miles per hour
the panic is encasing
i have no power

my body feels numb
the storm is too wild
where did it come from?
my emotions are piled

neatly packed thoughts become undone
for the true storm has only just begun

watching

people walk so fast
they rush to wherever they need to be
with faces rested
between smile and frown

what are their stories?
an average life?
a tough life?
life changing events?

some need to stop
to take a step back from the world
watch the people around them
learn from the actions of others

mornings

repetative rings alert me
a phone screen wakes me

showers soothe tension
dressing focuses my mind

the phone screen distracts
for minutes without end

time kept going
moving forward

when I open the front door
the day can finally begin

languages

yes, si, oui, oo
words that mean the same
but said in different ways

distinguishes who people are
where they come from
where they go

barriers and borders
letting people in
letting people out

when looking from the outside
you cannot understand
if you don't speak the tongue of the land

words open you to culture
to different ways of life
from all around the world

but do not judge on words themselves
for similar words cross between languages
sounding the same, meaning different things

bringing us together
keeping us apart
all beautiful in their own way

life

twenty years
lovers
sitting on the steps
it pours over everything
thirty years, we live together
the light goes out and the hot water does not work
naked
i'm ashamed
thirty-five
the arm along the body
i pressed between my fingers
awake
fifty
we are not together anymore
we never meet
separated
we are a thousand years old
foot, stone, nose, sand
matter is converted
we exist

waiting

staying in and making no plans
laying on the couch, car keys in hand
constant glances at my phone
hoping to hear your ringtone

hope gleaming from my doe-eyes
ignoring all of your lies
sitting and getting nothing done
because my heart has already been won

all the empty promises
time spent that is missed
constantly waiting for you
to come and do what you said you'd do

clothes

jeans don’t fit
shirt's too tight
something here isn’t right

is it me?
am i the problem?
NO

clothes made for one body
a universal standard that so few fit
while the rest are left in the dust

look around
find one person that has the same body as you
seeking the impossible

an exclusive society
making people vulnerable
preying on the vulnerable

everything is right with you
the clothes are in the wrong

you

chocolate brown hair, wild and fun
amber eyes that shine in the sun
slanted smile that makes me warm
one dimple in man-made form

13, we met
first period math
16, we kissed
that created our path

20, now
still going strong
3 years and counting
it was always you all along

billions of people in this world
but you chose me to hold and twirl
around as we dance
through our own love story romance

woman

woman
a fearless force of nature
carrying the weight of the world
while setting the dinner table

woman
powerful and strong
bringing life onto earth
and keeping things aesthetic

woman
capable of anything
easy and impossible
yet always undermined

woman
problem solvers
creative thinkers
but never accredited for their genius

woman
the backbones of society
the brightness of the future
now we rise

woman
a fearless force of nature

strings

strings pull from my depth
every part of you i cannot forget

yes or no?
a question of heart or soul

strings tug at the worst part of me
but there is more that what others see

you and i
me and you
to do or don't
an answer i never knew

books

the encapsulating smell of parchment
the familiar feel of cover and binding
the curiosity of a first sentence
the anticipation of the climax
the adventure of a journey

life changing lessons written between lines
these are the consuming parts of books
addicting qualities that make an underdog the
heroin
a place where the odd fit in

change

the security of certainty
beginning to dwindle away

what once was
no longer is

what is now
will not be tomorrow

actions ripple
down the passage of time

all takes its toll
on the fate of life

for time does not stop moving
the world does not stop changing

but i stand here
still and resistant

constant movement intimidates
uncertainty daunts

watching every sense go on
seems to be satisfactory

do i desire to be left in the dust?
do i wish to be stuck in yesterday?

adaptation and adjustment
both necessities for life

for growth should be achieved
progress should be made

sunshine

i used to sit in the darkness waiting
waiting for someone to notice me while i cry for no help
i guess i found comfort in being alone by then
but you ruined that

you flashed a bright light in my face
it was surprising, i didn't know what to do
but it was the first light i had seen in months

so i accepted it and walked towards it
people usually say that walking towards the light meant death
but what i found was the opposite

as i got closer my eyes began to adjust
i saw you

i love you
you saved me when there was no hope
you loved me when i had forgotten what love felt like
you shine like a star bigger than any other
you are the sun
you are my sunshine

parents

people who want to populate the earth
signing up for life long job
that begins before child birth

clueless and scared
learning along the way
just trying to show how much they care

mistakes are often made
and many bumps in the road are hit
that can affect the way their love is displayed

as children grow older
becoming their own person
the shoulder they give can seem much colder

but bonds between kin are hard to break
no matter how bruised and battered
only so much negativity a heart can take

a special kind of love
typically overlooked and taken for granted
can rise above

growth

growth, a constant in life
starting as thoughtless babies
ending as thoughtful elders

time moves
never slows down
no time to stop and smell the roses

grade school to high school
high school to college
college to real life

thinking we know it all at each stage
but never knowing anything in reality

when do we know?
when do we find the secret to life?
when do we figure it out?

never
never
never

omniscience is infeasible
an open mind and awareness
those are attainable

to live life to its fullest
growth, a constant in life

www.ingramcontent.com/pod-product-compliance
Lightning Source LLC
Chambersburg PA
CBHW051720130826
49812CB00034B/1277
* 9 7 8 9 3 5 7 2 1 3 0 1 1 *